**JUST
US
TWO**

To Jim, companion of my heart,
and our beloved sons Eli and Gabriel.
Joyce Sidman

For my Dad, Arnold
Susan Swan

"Along the Nile" previously appeared in Cricket Magazine.

Photographs courtesy of © Tim Davis: p. 28 (top); Photo Researchers, Inc.: pp. 28
(© Cosmos Blank, center), 29 (© Jeanne White, top; © Gregory G. Dimijian, M.D. 1986,
bottom), 30 (©Nigel J. Dennis, top); Minden Pictures: pp. 28 (© Mitsuaki Iwago, bottom),
30 (© Jim Brandenburg, center); Visuals Unlimited: p. 29 (© Parke H. John, Jr., center);
Peter Arnold, Inc.: p. 30 (© Kathy Watkins, bottom); Auscape International: p. 31 (© John
Cancalosi, top); Animals Animals: p. 31 (© J. Clare, bottom)

Published by The Millbrook Press, Inc.
2 Old New Milford Road
Brookfield, CT 06804
www.millbrookpress.com

Library of Congress Cataloging-in-Publication Data
Sidman, Joyce.
Just us two : poems about animal dads / Joyce Sidman;
cut-paper illustrations by Susan Swan.
p. cm.
Summary: Eleven poems present life from the point of view of
various animal fathers and their young, including Emperor penguins, Nile crocodiles, and giant
water bugs.
ISBN 0-7613-1563-2 (lib. bdg.)
1. Parental behavior in animals—Juvenile poetry. 2. Father
and child—Juvenile poetry. 3. Children's poetry, American.
4. Parenting—Juvenile poetry. 5. Fathers—Juvenile poetry.
[1. Animals—Infancy—Poetry. 2. Father and child—Poetry.
3. American poetry.] I. Swan, Susan Elizabeth, ill. II. Title. PS3569.I295J87   2000
811'.54—dc21   98-51454   CIP AC

Copyright © 2000 by Joyce Sidman
Cut-Paper Illustrations copyright © 2000 by Susan Swan
Original art photographed by Terry Rasberry
Printed in the United States of America
5 4 3 2 1

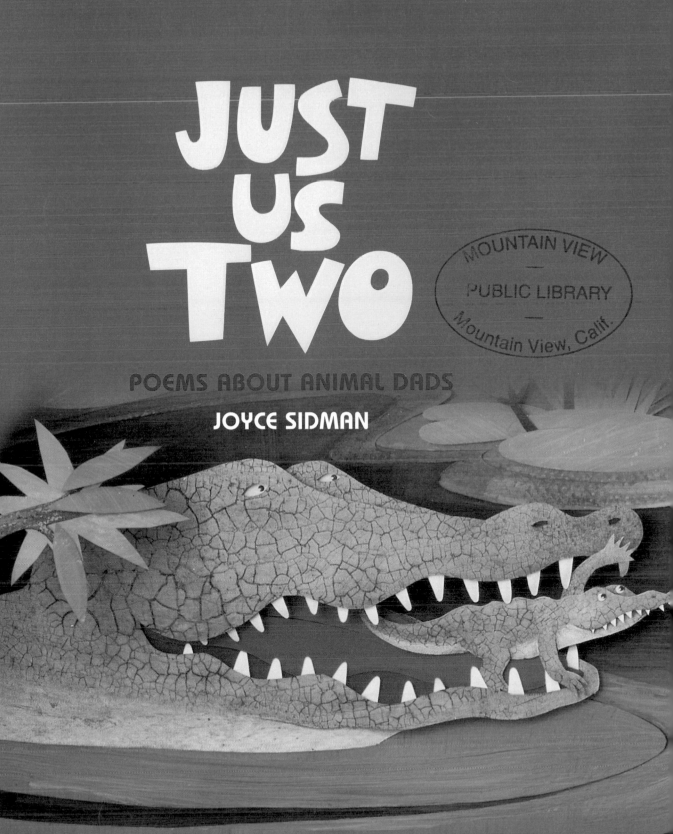

JUST US TWO

POEMS ABOUT ANIMAL DADS

JOYCE SIDMAN

Cut-Paper Illustrations by Susan Swan

The Millbrook Press   Brookfield, Connecticut

IF I
WERE AN
EGG

If I
were an egg,
I'd be a Big Daddy
Emperor Penguin Egg.
Round and fat on Big Daddy
feet, under folds of fluff from
Big Daddy belly. Let the cold
wind howl and the snow blow
sideways! It wouldn't touch
me: Big Daddy's Big Bad
Emperor Penguin-to-be.

EGG BUSINESS

Busy, busy:
I've got eggs.
Real tight schedule:
I've got eggs.
Up at dawn
to clean the eggs.
Deep-knee bends
to rinse the eggs.
Swim up top
to warm the eggs.
Dive down fast
to hide the eggs.
Sit in sun
to dry the eggs.

Life is tough
when you've got eggs.
Sometimes all I see are eggs!
Heavy, tickly, twisty eggs.
Squirmy, wormy,
    hatching eggs.
Swimming, scooting,.

                    scramming eggs.

Empty eggs.
What to do?

Need more eggs.

SONG OF THE NIGHT

I AM ANCIENT,
TWO-TOED,
HEAVY-BONED.
I AM FATHER.

I am tiny,
curled-up,
cooped and cramped.
I am egg.

MY NEST
IS MY STRONGHOLD.
ALONE, IN THE DARK,
I WATCH AND WAIT.

My shell
is my prison.
Alone, in the dark,
I call out.

WHAT IS
THIS SOFT RUMBLE
BENEATH MY FEET?

What is
this loud chatter
above my head?

CLACK! CLACK!
CLACK! CLACK!

Peep! Peep!
Peep! Peep!

SO MANY CALLING,
A CHORUS OF NESTLINGS!

So many tapping,
a clamor of crackling!

UNDER MY BEAK,
SOFT WET FEATHERS
SHIVER AND HATCH.

Overhead
huge warm wings
blanket and shelter.

CLACK! CLACK!   CLACK! CLACK!

WELCOME.
I AM FATHER.
I AM YOURS.

Father.
I am . . . me.
I am yours.

Peep! Peep!   Peep! Peep!

BUDGIE BABIES

Budgie babies slumber soundly,
snoring slightly through their beaks,
brothers, sisters, all a jumble,
stomachs growling in their sleep.

Dad appears with seeds a-plenty;
budgies wake and open wide.
Who will get dear Daddy's goodies?
He who makes the loudest cry.

Budgie babies bellow boldly,
brawl and babble, screech and squeal,
push and pummel brothers, sisters,
for a tasty budgie meal.

Such a ruckus! Such a rumpus!
Such a loud, ear-splitting din!
Daddy stuffs with nerves a-jangle,
flees as fast as he flew in.

Budgie babies burp and burble,
sigh and settle, sniff and snort.
Some are full and some are hungry,
all are just a little hoarse.

Budgie babies slumber soundly,
snoring slightly through their beaks.
Brothers, sisters, all a jumble
dream of Daddy in their sleep.

MOUSE HAIKU

Blind and tissue-skinned,
tiny mice enter the world
in a nest of grass.

Hide-and-seek masters,
they will soon whisk, surefooted,
through the chill spring night.

Until then, Father
warms this fragile thimbleful
of fluttering hearts.

FROGGY-BACK

This little froglet never has to beg or plead with daddy frog to slow those giant dadlike hops so he can keep in step. Out from his tiny mushroom egg he pops, and knows just where to head: the sticky, slimy, bright and shiny back that waits for him. And, daddy-back, he gloms right on

and tours the jungle's tangled green
and never has to leave at all
until he gets the urge
to slide into a dewy pool
of water neither warm nor cool:
in short, a spot exactly right
for slipping off his daddy's back
and stretching out his froggy legs
to swim all on his froggy own.

ALONG THE NILE

What delight
to swim along the oozy, snoozy Nile
to swing my tail from side to side,

stretch my pop-up eyeballs w i d e ,

dunk and splash and dive and glide

along the oozy, snoozy, deep and cruisy Nile.

I am a spy
that lurks along the oozy, snoozy Nile.

Among the rushes thick and deep
I listen to the plovers peep,

I watch the hippo-mamas sleep

I slink and crawl and crouch and c r e e p

along the oozy, cruisy,

oh-so-snoozy Nile.

Then the dikkop starts to cry!

The hippos **shriek**

the plovers fly!

A hyena looks me in the eye!

Umph-umph-umph!

I grunt in fear.

Will Papa's toothy jaws a p p e a r

to scoop me up and out of here?

I am a prince

who rides along the oozy, cruisy Nile.
Away up in my royal seat
'twixt kingly teeth so large and neat
I wave my tail to all I meet,
I nod and bow and call and greet
along the oozy, cruisy,

not-
so-

snoozy Nile.

RULES OF THE PACK

Nose low, tail high.

      Nose low, tail high.

Paws down, ears up.

      Paws down, ears up.

Sniff and pounce.

      Sniff and pounce.

Stick together.

      Stick together.

I'm the boss.

      You're the boss.

Yip means happy.

        Yip means happy.

Howl means come.

        Howl means come.

Respect your elders.

        Respect my elders.

No biting my tail.

        No biting your—chomp!

I said no biting!

        But, Dad, it's twitching!

Respect your elders!

        But, Dad, it's fun!

I'll roll you over . . .

        Wheeeee! Do it again!

You silly cub!

        Again, again!

Okay, lesson's over.

        Except for one.

What do you mean?

        Cubs like to play.

Cubs like to play!

Dads do, too.

FLYING LESSON

This time, Father says,
he will not bring me my dinner.
This time
he will let it fall,
and I must try to catch it.

Flying, Father says,
is like seeing the air.
Not just the blue shimmer,
not just the bright clouds,
but the air itself
as it swells and swirls
around our rocky cliff.

To show me,
he leaps from the nest,
gathers the wind in his wings,
and dives.
He comes up dangling dinner
between his claws.

He calls to me:
Now! Fly!

Because I love him,
because he says to,
because I want with all my heart
to catch that bait,
I tumble out:
flapping,
dropping,
s o a r i n g
into the blue, shimmering air
that I can almost see.

DOING THE ROCK-HOP SKITTER

Up on the kopje, way up high,
Daddy says, with a watchful eye:
"Keep your hooves in the air
                    and your ears to the sky
when you're doing the Rock-Hop Skitter."

Those flatlanders, they don't know squat
'bout what it really takes to trot
up mountain cliffs,
                    down lava rock,
doing the Rock-Hop Skitter.

Compared to most, we're mighty small,
and leopards sure look fast and tall,
but Dad says
                    we'll outrun 'em all
if we do that ol' Rock-Hop Skitter.

First, he says, you point your toes,
cock your head and strike a pose,
flare that cute

                black-button nose,
before doing the Rock-Hop Skitter.

Hear a noise? Catch a sniff
of something creeping up that cliff?
Don't you stop

                to wonder if—
Start doing the Rock-Hop Skitter.

Tuck those legs up under you,
kick out hard and fast and true . . .
Hey, that's it—

                I almost flew!
I'm doing the Rock-Hop Skitter!

Up on the kopje, way up high,
here we are, just Dad and I,
hooves in the air

                and ears to the sky,
doing the Rock-Hop Skitter!

HANGIN'

Mom's a mess.
Dad says she's tired.
You'd be tired, too,
he says, if you'd lugged
a kid that long
inside of YOU.

So let's take off, I say.
Let's go hangin'.

I lock on all four feet
with my roller-coaster grip
and we're gone!

Hangin' .

Dad's the best at tree to tree,
so fast sometimes
I close my eyes.

Not today.
I'm lookout.
Good thing, too,
'cause looped above us
I see something
on a branch:
half vine, half Bad.

Snake! I croak.

Dad lets out a scream
that scares that sorry snake
half-silly.
And we're gone.
Outta there.

Hangin'.
Just us two.
Hangin' all day long.

EMPEROR PENGUIN

Emperor penguins live in one of the coldest places on earth: Antarctica. After the mother lays an egg, the father rolls it on top of his feet and snuggles it under his feathered belly-flap. This protects the egg from the ice and freezing temperatures. For two long, bitter months, father penguins stand huddled in a group without eating, until the eggs hatch and the mother penguins return. Then Mom takes over and Dad goes out to sea to fish for a much-needed meal.

GIANT WATER BUG

Giant water bugs live in ponds all across North America. In most species, the mother bug lays her eggs right on her mate's inch-long back. She also releases a kind of glue that sticks them firmly in place. From then on, it's up to Dad to care for the hundred or so eggs, which he cleans, oxygenates, and guards from predators. After twelve days, the eggs hatch and the baby water bugs swim away.

OSTRICH

On the hot, dry plains of Africa, the male ostrich scrapes a shallow hole in the dirt. Into this hollow, the female lays up to fifteen of the largest eggs in the world—nearly eight inches long! The mother sits on the eggs by day, and the father sits on them at night. When either parent hears a faint peeping from the nest, they call back to encourage their nestlings to hatch.

AUSTRALIAN BUDGERIGAR PARAKEET

You have probably seen a budgerigar, or "budgie," in a pet store, for they are one of the most common kinds of caged bird. In the wild, they live in large flocks on the grasslands of Australia. During the rainy season when there is plenty of food, the mother budgerigar lays eggs as often as possible. This means there are sometimes brothers and sisters of different sizes and ages in the nest at one time. Both parents feed the young hatchlings, but while the mother tends to feed each baby equally, research has shown that the father budgie often quiets the loudest baby first with a mouthful of food!

CALIFORNIA DEER MOUSE

California deer mice are often born during the coldest months of the year. They are only one-and-a-half inches long, without fur, and completely helpless. They do not even open their eyes until two weeks have gone by! The father mouse stays with the mother and babies, using his protective warmth to shield them against the cold, rainy weather. Although he cannot nurse his young, he performs all other parental duties, including cleaning their small bodies with his tongue.

TWO-TONED POISON-ARROW FROG

Deep in the rain forests of South America, mother poison-arrow frogs lay their eggs. The brightly colored father guards them. When the eggs hatch, Dad stands still as the baby frogs scramble onto his back. They attach themselves with suckerlike mouths and catch a free ride until they are big enough to swim on their own.

NILE CROCODILE

Most reptiles forget about their eggs as soon as they are laid. The Nile crocodile, however, keeps watch over its nest and carefully carries its babies to the water after they hatch. A baby crocodile, weighing less than a pound, may be 4,000 times smaller than its full-grown mother or father! Nonetheless, crocodile junior can safely ride in papa's enormous jaws if danger threatens.

ARCTIC WOLF

Each spring, when the ice and snow of the Arctic gives way to grass and flowers, the arctic wolf pack stops roaming and finds a den. After the wolf cubs are born, the life of the pack centers around them. Parents, aunts, uncles, and siblings watch over the cubs, teach them, and bring food back to them. They are like a large, loving family with a strong leader—the cub's father, called the Alpha Male. He leads the hunts, watches for danger, and occasionally takes time out to do what all wolves love to do: play.

PEREGRINE FALCON

To catch their prey, peregrine falcons dive from great heights, at speeds up to 236 miles per hour. Such skills are not easily learned, and young falcons spend a period of about two months in "flight school" before they leave the nest completely. One way fathers teach is to drop food from above. The young falcon tries to catch it in midair, but if he doesn't, mama falcon is waiting below. She snags the food, flies up, and drops it again for another try.

KLIPSPRINGER ANTELOPE

These South African antelopes stand only two feet tall but are expert climbers. In fact, their name means "cliff-hopper" in Afrikaans ("kopje" means "hill"). Klipspringers can leap up slippery rocks on their special "tiptoe" hooves. They stay with their mates for life, standing guard for each other while grazing on berries, seeds, and evergreen bushes. Babies are born in a hidden cave or rocky outcropping. After hiding out for three months with Mom, baby klipspringers are ready to hit the slopes with Dad, to learn how to do some "cliff hopping!"

SOUTH AMERICAN TITI MONKEY

About the only time baby titi monkeys see their moms is at mealtime. After they are done nursing, they climb back onto Dad, who seems to have the most patience in this monkey family. Even when they are old enough to find their own food in the rain forests of South America, young titis stick with Dad, either catching a ride on his back or snuggling next to him with tails entwined.

the end

ABOUT THE AUTHOR AND ILLUSTRATOR

JOYCE SIDMAN became interested in animal dads while reading to her children about the fascinating ways animals shelter, feed, and teach their young. As she watched her husband and sons at their home in Minnesota, she noticed many similarities between animal families and human ones! More study led her to the conclusion that many fathers in the wild are not the ferocious creatures we think they are. Like human fathers, they are protective, nurturing, and critical to the survival of their offspring.

For *Just Us Two* SUSAN SWAN created three-dimensional cut-paper artwork. First she selected her papers and hand painted them to get the colors and textures she needed for each poem. Then she went to work creating each piece of art, layering the papers to accomplish the dramatic sense of depth that gives such life to each piece of art. Finally, Susan's husband, Terry, photographed the finished artwork, with lighting that accents the shadows of the paper. Susan and her husband are, professionally, Swan & Rasberry Studios, and they live in Texas.